SIX O'CLOCK MINE REPORT

Six O'Clock Mine Report

Irene McKinney

University of Pittsburgh Press

Published by the University of Pittsburgh Press, Pittsburgh, Pa. 15260
Copyright © 1989, Irene McKinney
All rights reserved
Feffer and Simons, Inc., London
Manufactured in the United States of America

Library of Congress Cataloging in Publication Data

McKinney, Irene.
Six o'clock mine report / Irene McKinney.
p.   cm. —(Pitt poetry series)
ISBN 0-8229-3611-9.   ISBN 0-8229-5415-X (pbk.)
I. Title. II. Series.
PS3633.A31756S5   1989
811'.54—dc19   88-29084
                                                              CIP

The author and publisher would like to thank the following publications in which some of the poems in this collection first appeared: *Black Warrior Review, Higginson Journal, Ironwood, Kayak, Laurel Review, North American Review, Poetry, Quarry West, Quarterly West, Trellis,* and *Western Humanities Review.*

"The Dance" first appeared in the *Cimarron Review* and is reprinted here with the permission of the Board of Regents for Oklahoma State University, holders of the copyright. The poem was also reprinted in *The Best of Cimarron Review,* an anthology. Copyright © 1981 by the Board of Regents of Oklahoma State University.

"Starlings in the Walls at Night" was originally published in *Northwest Review.*

*The publication of this book is supported by grants
from the National Endowment for the Arts
in Washington, D.C., a Federal agency,
and the Pennsylvania Council on the Arts.*

for
My mother, Celia Durrett
and
My father, Ralph Durrett

Contents

Contents

I

Six O'Clock Mine Report

Twilight in West Virginia: Six O'Clock Mine Report

Bergoo Mine No. 3 will work: Bergoo Mine
No. 3 will work tomorrow. Consol. No. 2
will not work: Consol. No. 2 will not
work tomorrow.

Green soaks into the dark trees.
The hills go clumped and heavy
over the foxfire veins
at Clinchfield, One-Go, Greenbrier.

At Hardtack and Amity the grit
abrades the skin. The air is thick
above the black leaves, the open mouth
of the shaft. A man with a burning

carbide lamp on his forehead
swings a pick in a narrow corridor
beneath the earth. His eyes flare
white like a horse's, his teeth glint.

From his sleeves of coal, fingers
with black half-moons: he leans
into the tipple, over the coke oven
staining the air red, over the glow

from the rows of fiery eyes at Swago.
Above Slipjohn a six-ton lumbers down
the grade, its windows curtained with soot.
No one is driving.

The roads get lost in the clotted hills,
in the Blue Spruce maze, the red cough,
the Allegheny marl, the sulphur ooze.

The hill-cuts drain; the roads get lost
and drop at the edge of the strip job.
The fires in the mines do not stop burning.

3

Potts Farm, Summer 1955

Faint smells of violet, bleach, cheese.
The starched doilies sag
on the arms of the horsehair sofa.
Aunt Floss is baking bread and laughing,
clacking her false teeth.

The house breathes smoke of bitter locust,
and Uncle Branch sits grinning, on and on,
spitting into the fire.
Night clots in the corner
with the smoke, with the yellow pages

of books, the green and eggshell cretonne,
and my grandmother floats in her rocker
and moves back and forth all afternoon.
All afternoon, and the rinsed haze
lifts from the cut grass and peonies

fleshing in clumps along the wire fence.
It's time now for the mailman
leaving in his tattered jeep.
It's time for us to call the cows
who are waiting below

in the printed mud by the pond,
time for the imperceptible chaff to fall,
and the hay to shift in the barn.

The Ruined House of the Photographer

Among the stones of the foundation,
copperheads in their slick chain mail
listen through delicate bones, and ferns.
Three-gallon stone jars in the caved-in kitchen
have cracked open from the pressure of expanding ice,
falling in shards on tarnished spoons and china figurines,
families of collies and deer.

In the closet, overalls and molting furs in strings,
one hundred hand-painted silk ties packed in mouse droppings.
And shuffling on the hearth, in broken drawers,
in sooty cabinets, are grainy photographs
of the eccentric dead. A seven-year-old girl,
her blonde hair prinked in a misshapen halo,
is painted like a fever, high spots

of powder pink on her smooth cheeks,
lips touched outside their outline,
the staring drills of impossible blue eyes.
She waits like the dead, too, for nothing,
or maybe for us to stumble onto the soggy threshold
and listen, standing at the foot of the stairwell
clogged up with pieces of the roof.

The photographer has a sequence of himself
smoking a cigar. Looking for chronology,
we see that in the first shot
he has not yet taken the cigar;
in the second he has, and is properly
pinching it with buff-colored fingers.
In the third there's an aura of smoke swirls

around his head, and now he's faintly smiling.
In the last full-face, the cigar is gone
again, and the man has grown thoughtful.
These pictures are at the bottom
of the stack, under the one
of the bald, big-headed child,
someone's ugly, beloved grief.

Starlings in the Walls at Night

A hunger like morning waking has entered with
the wind from the chimney and hovered over the dead fire; it
   wants
to come out somewhere, some opening, any chink of entry.
Driven this way, the lice on its wings are agitated, believing
the starling has gone to sleep, moving toward the eyes.
For a moment, the starling is tranced, believing that too;
the lids of thin leather flicker and close for an instant,

and then it drops shuddering in the walls. Below it, beside it,
I'm burrowing through the dark of my half sleep, half listening
to the wind take the loose boards again, knowing that the birds
are passing through, around the frayed wiring, scratching at
the chimney fissures, leaving lice and droppings in a scramble
to find out exactly where they are. And I get up, as I've done
for many nights, entered from within and without, having become

a place of many crossings, thread-paths of bird-track, bat-weave,
spider-center, moth-goal: no outside lights and so they flock
to windows, neglected porch and flaking wood tell them no one's
there. But I am, like a seed hidden inside the garden, here
for many months to get away. There are six, seven starlings
now, the feathers sifting in the walls, the old bones gathering
webs and soot. I'm standing in the middle of the room, my feet

chilling on the bare boards, birds in my blood, on my hair.
The sound of straw and sticks, the nesting. And I am tranced
and populated to choking, the work and friends I left to be alone
are nothing to compare with this weaving of scuddering lives,
these creatures unsymboled, emerging from the earth and air
to take their place wherever there's an opening, any size
or shape. And morning comes to generate more eggs and seeds.

Before Spring

After two weeks of beginnings, spring has not happened
again, although *The Handbook of the Insect World* tells me

that this big bumbling bee who fell in
through the open door with a nimbus of cool air

does not arrive till spring does. If the bee
could read such things, he would feel as I do—

inexact, out-of-place, inappropriate again
in my bad timing and repeated, cyclic lack

of synchronization. The way I said in a clumsy
reflex of belief that someone I spoke to

was just wrong, all wrong, should go away
and begin to think in a different way entirely,

become someone else more complicated. And my belief
in that was struggling out of season, the time I find

myself a part of, and it isn't spring again.
Nothing quite emerges, but it pushes up

because our deepest urges need
to come out in season. If the bee that blundered

in here had kept on growing inside his little hexagon
he would have squeezed himself to death just

by continuing. Like that, the rooms I find myself inside
are odd-shaped and functional, for a while.

A *Freshet in Brattleboro*

I stepped off the bus in Brattleboro, Vermont,
uncramping my cold knees and smoothing down
my good brown skirt, and walked away
from the oily fumes over the gravelly lot
and wondered, what could I do for an hour.
The only way for someone like me
who has no patience is to assume it,
and I've practiced. So I went to the edge
of the pavement where a clear gray stream of water
had broken out of the side of winter
and flowed along according to its wont
past broken cars, and trees, and didn't pause.
I knew it had burst out and the only thing
to do was to watch it, so I folded my legs
and sat on a newspaper and gave myself up
to the stream. And God I was so grateful,
I thought, how can I stumble around
this world everyday always wanting something?
I still did, but it was different. The water
purled and eddied and moved on
with intention, but what that intention
is cannot be thought of, exactly,
but only sat beside, by someone like me,
who finds it hard to talk about it.

Phoebe, Phoebe, Phoebe

Oh you sweet birds. I heard your voices trilling
and I figured the day wasn't lost at all,
although you don't even know me. That you're here,
you've arrived, is amazing, and coming from *reptiles?*
If that's so, then I don't know how I've lived this long
in such darkness. Come on out, then, and make
that sound you make, that series of sounds,
so incomprehensible and so straight, full
of solids and liquids and your knowledge
of the depths of the sea, which you've translated
into tides of air. That's another world up there,
currents flowing, great storms, huge landscapes,
airscapes, invisible forever to me. The way it
is to live there I can hear through you, jays,
sparrows, phoebes, chickadees, who passed back
and forth all winter long like a parallel
universe, though you sweet birds know nothing
of me and my strange heart. It makes me
want to listen, and keep the lines of our
worlds in tandem. I try to fly here
in these odd ways, while you are warbling
that liquid from the other sea.

Little Boats

When I wake up, I slide
my hand across my eyes
to find them, with a vague
affection, the way you put
your hand on my breast as
I pass, and you go on reading your book.

I have lost whole lives, and such
strokes keep this one.
Once, I floated across a meadow
like a leaf on a stream
or a cell in the blood,
but now I'm near the ocean.

I chose to be near this sound.
This afternoon, I took a walk
out to its lip, and some cormorants
wheeled and cried. I stood at a phone
and called you, and while we talked
I looked out over soft brown grass,

toward the water. The horizon line
leapt up in fiery pink. And I
think if I can go on leading
lives like this one down
to the ocean, they will set
in their little boats, and be recovered.

Deep Mining

Think of this: that under the earth
there are black rooms your very body

can move through. Just as you always
dreamed, you enter the open mouth

and slide between the glistening walls,
the arteries of coal in the larger body.

I knock it loose with the heavy hammer.
I load it up and send it out

while you walk up there on the crust,
in the daylight, and listen to the coal-cars

bearing down with their burden.
You're going to burn this fuel

and when you come in from your chores,
rub your hands in the soft red glow

and stand in your steaming clothes
with your back to it, while it soaks

into frozen buttocks and thighs.
You're going to do that for me

while I slog in the icy water
behind the straining cars.

Until the swing-shift comes around.
Now, I am the one in front of the fire.

Someone has stoked the cooking stove
and set brown loaves on the warming pan.

Someone has laid out my softer clothes,
and turned back the quilt.

Listen: there is a vein that runs
through the earth from top to bottom

and both of us are in it.
One of us is always burning.

Sunday Morning, 1950

Bleach in the foot-bathtub.
The curling iron, the crimped, singed hair.
The small red marks my mother makes
across her lips.

Dust in the road, and on the sumac.
The tight, white sandals on my feet.

In the clean sun before the doors,
the flounces and flowered prints,
the naked hands. We bring
what we can—some coins,
our faces.

The narrow benches we don't fit.
The wasps at the blue hexagons.

And now the rounding of the unbearable
vowels of the organ, the O
of release. We bring
some strain, and lay it down
among the vowels and the gladioli.

The paper fans. The preacher paces,
our eyes are drawn to the window,
the elms with their easy hands.

Outside, the shaven hilly graves we own.
Durrett, Durrett, Durrett. The babies there
that are not me. Beside me,
Mrs. G. sings like a chicken
flung in a pan on Sunday morning.

. . . This hymnal I hold in my hands.
This high bare room, this strict accounting.
This rising up.

II

The Only Portrait of Emily Dickinson

The Only Portrait of Emily Dickinson

The straight neck held up out of the lace
is bound with a black velvet band.
She holds her mouth the way she chooses,
the full underlip constrained by a small muscle.

She doesn't blink or look aside,
although her left eye is considering
a slant. She would smile
if she had time, but right now

there is composure to be invented.
She stares at the photographer.
The black crepe settles. Emerging
from the sleeve, a shapely hand

holds out a white, translucent blossom.
"They always say things which embarrass
my dog," she tells the photographer.
She is amused, but not as much as he'd like.

Her Fascicles

The light on this page is not bright,
but the light in my mind is.

I felt for a scrap, a guarantee
from a Chimney Gallery lamp

and flipped it over in the dark.
The moon slid far off above everything.

I couldn't see.
I grasped the pen as hard as I could

and wrote four lines:
in the morning I saw they overlapped

but this was the thing itself
and I let it be.

I put it in a packet
with the others: the Chocalat Meunier wrapper,

the mildewed subscription blank,
the soiled brown paper bags smoothed out,

and tucked them all in a little drawer
where I can stretch out my hand

and touch them any time I want to.

She Speaks of Her Sister

Vinnie loves me, I believe. I pass up the back stairs
and over her head as I go down the hall to my room.
I lock the door and sit at the clean oak desk.
Vinnie was reading the paper and having her morning tea.
She will see that no one disturbs me,

and when Mag comes to clean, she'll tell her to knock,
and leave the cleaning if I'm occupied.
She'll say the things I can't be bothered to say.
She'll look the way I can't be bothered to look.
She sees sharp but not deep, but Vinnie loves me, I believe.

The Birds

Their bones are full of air. I know they are something
beyond us all, yet I must touch this in some way.
I want to feel the tiny body in my hand,
the steady faint fluttering, the soft wispy feathers.

I am familiar with the ones I'll never know.
I feel their little hearts with me always.
I come as near their speech as anyone can,
and yet they fly away, and will not talk.

On a July morning, they move in the outside air
as I can not. They coast at ease
in their riding. They loop and present
themselves, and pass over.

I take notes and enter their names.
I draw near, but can't touch them. I say hello,
but my tongue twists as though the words
were Aramaic or Senegalese. The air hurts

my bones: my arches bend high and don't quite
touch down, my hair glints bright and wisps in the wind,
and my heart loses weight. I have carried my flowers
and cups to them also. And now they pass over, pass over.

Her Name

The name they dropped upon my face,
the shape they tried to give my eyes,
the hands they handed me,
the kinds of shoes, the aprons.

I will not pretend to see less than I do
to make them comfortable, nor dissemble for love,
to feel less severe than I do when standing in a field
of green alfalfa hearing the wood dove call.

So many, three now, I wanted to touch in their centers,
to hear them say the words that open the stops,
but they waited for a bending without knowing they waited,
looked at me much because I gave them a shock

they found nowhere else in their lives,
waited while I waited, and walked away,
finding their ease elsewhere.
I walked up the narrowing passage

to the room and sat at the writing table.
My hands got thin and pale, like moths,
she said. I knew she was married
but I called him the person you live with,

"the friend who is always with you."
And the one with a face like a burning lamp,
he was married yet I could not believe these forms
had any meaning and would not grant it

when I talked to them. If they felt such shining
in their minds and bodies as I looked at them,
if they wanted more and more
of what I could pour in their cups,

how could they not nod once and say to me—
not even in their language, but some way
say to me that they acknowledged the receiving?
This I could not believe would not happen,

do not believe will not happen.
Fruits and flowers, the best ripe plums,
the Indian Pipe found in the coolest spot,
the hothouse blooms forced up

out of their tight roots into a precise blooming.
These emblems I give to you: the mouth,
the vulva, and the brain.
Of course you knew, you all knew

what I had given you.
You could not not know. And I will
continue and endure in my unbelief.

Her Poem

You could have eased me some—
When I—caught in a Gyre—
With shaking hands—and numb
To all but my desire—
Clenched tight around a fire—
That seared me to the bone—
Myself—a living Pyre—
The fault of it—My own—

And you—afraid of burning—
Turned—and would not see—
I could not keep from turning—
Oh—you could have eased me.

She Says Zero

I have never been seduced. I am always myself.
You cannot prevent me from choosing
to love you in my way. I choose to love
what shines out of you, and not
the doors you close against that light.

I will never love your breakfast cups, your cravats,
your uses in the world. You cannot seduce me.
I would meet you in that open space
at the center where the real words pulse,
where the meaning is.

I will hold out my hands to you
at the same moment yours are
extended, palms-up.
But I will not be seduced.
No. Zero.

She Speaks to the Visitor
at the Dickinson Homestead

Lavinia knows, and the crock in the pantry,
and the tabby, and Mrs. Luke Sweetser,
and Sister Sue. They know because
I am with them now, as I was before.

In the sign of the goldenrod, and the black yew,
in the closed cloud signatures—buttermilk,
mare's tail, gray scud—they know.
As they lie at the side of Amity Street

they soak up your footprints and they know.
You, on the other side, are one of the pilgrims
who come here, gazing down Main Street
past the Homestead and the mossed path,

finding your directions. You do not know
as I do how Maggie and Abiah and Tom
in his blue jacket thrive in the sod
and adjust the ground. You come here

and listen to the sough in the pines,
the creak in the rafter, and rain,
and lay down your names on the leaves
of the house. You leave me notes

and I do not read them, you give over
your books of dates and your sequence,
and I let them slip from my hands.
We don't grow safer, nor more dangerous

and we do not wait for you: Sam Bowles,
and Maria Whitney, Reverend Jenkins,
and Austin—we do not wait for you.
You stand at the high window, looking

over the church spire, and I let you;
you handle the cotton in the closet,
and I let you. You long for the face
and the voice, and I let you long,
and you say "What" to me.

III

Limited Access

Visiting My Gravesite:
Talbott Churchyard, West Virginia

Maybe because I was married and felt secure and dead
at once, I listened to my father's urgings about "the future"

and bought this double plot on the hillside with a view
of the bare white church, the old elms, and the creek below.

I plan now to use both plots, luxuriantly spreading out
in the middle of a big double bed. —But no,

finally, my burial has nothing to do with my marriage, this lying
    here
in these same bones will be as real as anything I can imagine

for who I'll be then, as real as anything undergone, going back
and forth to "the world" out there, and here to this one spot

on earth I really know. Once I came in fast and low
in a little plane and when I looked down at the church,

the trees I've felt with my hands, the neighbors' houses
and the family farm, and I saw how tiny what I loved or knew
    was,

it was like my children going on with their plans and griefs
at a distance and nothing I could do about it. But I wanted

to reach down and pat it, while letting it know
I wouldn't interfere for the world, the world being

everything this isn't, this unknown buried in the known.

No Elegy

Many of those days held no elegies.
Nights, the moon slid into our room

and we didn't care. You lifted me
against the wall and we were bathed

in heat and sweat that stirred
the silver light. We traveled up

and down the stairs on our hands
and knees. We labored, and clung

to each other like drowning dogs.
We choked and cried. I wanted

to hold onto your hand and be
your friend but I couldn't,

there was no teaching about it,
and though my mind stayed with us

my body didn't, it was thrashing
and getting lost minute by minute.

And that went on, and still does
in some red place in my mind.

When we gave it up, for a while
we chatted quietly, as though

the moon had never thrown
us around the room.

Pike County Breakdown

I've got my ache cut out for me,
leaning against the grain.
In these several colored pens
I make my mark: magenta, puce,
and lips juiced like an elderberry.
I've got to get my mind off
whoever I make a face for,
and he's everywhere. Somehow,
the air is swirling near my mouth
whenever I set out to speak
a word I thought once. It's easier
for him, and therefore terrible.
When I seem to be speaking
he seems to be listening.
It's time to take them back:
the red strap shoes, the apple-lips,
the cinnamon handbag, the pear-skin,
and the almond eyes. They will be
plucked and baked, believe it, do.
These fruits are mine: my house,
my body, and my boughs.
I'm pulling down the branch
to hold it in my lap.

A Stream in His Mind

Her hands, he thinks, are limp things
that don't work, the fingers perfectly
smooth and tapered and never used.
These are the fingers he wants to lick,
press against his groin which becomes

dark as a bull's when he sees it
beside that hand. What can she do?
She is a small gold feather he can
stroke himself with: her sloped child's
hips he would tenderly break, her thighs

like water in a stream. He enters a stream
in his mind that's brimming over.
The willow drops her hair. The green
split pod, the dramatic, terrible contrast.
He feels that he is happy. Lays her down.

To His Wife

There is no one else to be helpless
before me, and so it has to be you,
beloved wife, who is all things.
And so I slash your legs like tires,
jerk your head backwards until
you are no longer female with
that skinned face like some
grinning boy's.
I have tried to explain
that you must be all things even
when those things won't mesh, and so
this willfulness in you cuts the legs
from underneath my life.
When you
are lying on the floor
below me, when I have struck the breast
that feeds and fills me till I gag,
when you have begged me to stop
and I feel that I could, but I don't,
then, then, you have been all the things
I can't live without, and I can
fall on my knees beside you, burying
my face in the ground of your hair.

The Jewelry Box

I own a lot of jewelry but I never wear
the many-stranded chains, the turquoise bracelet,
the jade ear drops, the heavy Aztec ring,
or the single gray pearl. Though you might

see me digging through some of my beloved silks,
the black satin dress, the giddy yellow
peasant frock, the red blouse,
I never wear them.

Sometimes I sit here in the stillness
of the afternoon in front of the gray screen
of the television glazed with dust and wish
that I could've stayed in the house

of my parents, with the chiming clock,
and the cat with the cruel, innocent face.
She blinked slowly at the fire all evening
and it seems to me now, that she didn't

really care for any of us, though she sat
so softly in my mother's lap and purred
when it pleased her: if not, she left
and wandered upstairs where she knew all the

rooms and their close, hidden places.
If I stare at the blank screen long enough,
I can see the cat's face there.
She opened the mouse's head carefully
and laid its small white brains
on the blue and red Persian rug.

Rapt

This is the part where after a few minutes
the audience asks the time, thinks about dinner
and going off alone to contemplate all this.

The actor watches through a crack
in the shutter as his wife unfolds her creamy
legs and the young doctor smoulders and blazes

above her. The actor turns
from the window in a spasm of grief
and paces the long room in a shaft

of golden light. He takes too long
to reach the green brocaded armchair, where
he slumps with his face in his hands, too long.

What are we to do while we wait for his recovery?
We can listen to the drone of the swelling violins.
We can watch the clear flame of the lamp

flickering. It's excessive, this protraction
of something so readily apparent.
And what are we to do while he stares off

to the right at the white stucco wall, the round
milky globe in the center of the table, while
he considers his large blunt hands, while

nothing is being advanced? And isn't grief specific
to death, and not to such continued throbbing
in the body, such a slow pull on the action

of the heart? All of us wish we could
rise in a body and leave at this point.
After all, haven't we set ourselves up

for this to see what happens? And nothing
is happening, except he has retracted
himself across the long red rug, and is staring

through his fingers at the white bed across
the way, where his wife lies curled like
a sated child and the dark young man is getting

dressed. This grief endures as long as we
can imagine. We know he'll weep sooner
or later, that he'll blow out the lamp at some
point, and re-light it later in the night.

Chrysanthemums

You may want to cut them down. You may want to use a knife,
and pare the brown leaves away. Your hands will smell
of their deep yellow voices and funeral air.
We sat in the parlor and stared at the shrinking petals.
All of us did; it was the same funeral. You could
inhale that spiced air and be glad, as glad
as you ever were, or anyone could be, seeing

such perfect convolutions. If I handed you
this whole load of chrysanthemums could you take
the dark air, the pointed, spiny wealth
of ragged scent? The magenta ones, burnt crocus,
are whited at the tips. In my room today
I have gathered three water glasses full,
and two white cups of just blossoms.

I wanted them in here with me. I dragged them
into my cave. There are many more outside,
but that is another story. This is what I can have,
these clusteral visions, the very last of the year.
White, with a tiny mustard spot in the center,
magenta starfish out of the sea, and gold,
for all it's worth. And that is enough for now.

This is a room, made in the touching human custom,
with windows and doors. How pitiful this is.
We gather outside for lunch under the elm
surrounded by chrysanthemums. Inside, I change
the water every day and pour away the rank juice
seeping from the stems. Aunt Avah lay in her coffin
like a locust husk while we talked of our houses
and rooms and read the cards on the flowers.

Mary Shelley: The Miscarriage

Then there was nothing at the center
where the roundness was. He and Claire talked

half the night and I'm sure they're right to go on
after the other ticking stopped. I put it

in an earthen jar until tomorrow, although I know
we will not hold a service for a thing so small.

When I looked in its face and knew we had made it
between us I felt almost relieved it would never

grow to say the things I fear it might have.
When you create a thing you have to be in the world

with it always although it grows and grows
and this one's face so swollen and unformed

it may have struggled with the urge to speak
and grunted. It might have been huge,

out of control. I am so tender and exposed
in every place these thoughts abrade me

like a metal clamp. If he could make a life
from his own thoughts I'm sure he would, with Claire

or someone like the drowned one to admire. I have counted
the expenses once again, and now I can omit the milk.

After it happened and I dozed I dreamt that something
loomed, larger than life. There was

a moat around it, and I heard the drawbridge clank.
Now he and Claire are making tea, I hear the cups.

We will bury the poor little thing in the morning.

Limited Access

The white road winds and loops
and narrows down to a flavor
of burnt earth, the story of sunstone
and moonstone, an injunction to travel.
Some of us are dreaming of earth's sunflowers
and her blasts of forsythia, and that she
is not a she; inside this enormous
limited space, inside this mitosis
of light, the white road loops and spins
and trawls its load of stars.
The brothers and sisters of enormous flavors
live in their green houses, saying: Anise,
the cream inside the moon, sun butter,
black bread. These spasms, these burns.

Taking Hold

Water. Water. Water.
Slips through our hands, eases, wets our mouths.
Such a liquid voice issuing from a rock.
And it has mouths and lips of its own.
Much faster than fire it enters the chain
of our being, and doesn't offend our fishy nature.
Its maps are trickling where I want to go.

But to be taken hold of by fire is to be lifted
into another form, so you can't know where you've been.
We are liable to be eaten in that guise, but
nature loves to hide, and I do too.
I do, I love to hide between the flare and wash,
the burning and the drink. In that clarity,
taking hold in love, I feel both flame and balm,
taking the grip of the fire for granted, taking the water

in, since that's what I already am.

The Dance

At first she led them out onto the floor
and they wanted to leave this open place
where they were judged. They remembered
the tiny rooms and windows, the puzzles
and blocks, the humming that could fill
their heads when they sat alone and rocked
with their arms around their knees.
But she held the girl's hand and lifted it
as the music rose. The girl was smooth
and round and cleft like a peach, her
mongoloid eyes were cheerful and slant,
and she stumbled until she felt
the lift of the song.

And then she led the man whose hands
wanted to smash, one against the other,
to the girl, and raised their hands
together as the music came again.
She showed them how to ease into
the bend and sway, and left them.

And now a woman aged by a strange disease
is moving with a veil which has become
the wind she's watching toss her up and
up above her bony knees and bent back
in black tights. She knows the wave
grows, and the paralyzed who can only
move an eyelid are swung about in
their chairs by the mute, who smile
at them in joy that will not be named,
and is not only in the movement
but in the summoning-up and offering
to all who care to see
the self that hovered in the shadowy halls
and has now emerged with all

its marks and scars still on it,
held out for anyone to touch.
They lifted up their arms, they lifted
up their faces, Lord, and danced.

They know they are being watched
by the whole, who they felt they could
not be, who have turned to them now
that their light is pouring out, and
they dance so gently because it is
forever, now. The ones who came
to watch are joining, they enter
the gentle rain, it is rising and
falling on us.

We lifted up our arms, we lifted
up our damaged faces, Lord,
and danced.

Notes

p. 5 "The Ruined House of the Photographer" is dedicated to Jayne Anne Phillips.

p. 11 "Phoebe, Phoebe, Phoebe" is dedicated to A. B. Paulson.

p. 19 "The Only Portrait of Emily Dickinson" borrows from her statement to Higginson in a letter: "Of 'shunning Men and Women'—they talk of Hallowed things, aloud—and embarrass my Dog—." (Dickinson's *Letters*, Thomas Johnson and Theodora Ward, Harvard, 1958).

p. 31 "The name they dropped upon my face" and "the friend who is always with you" are phrases from Dickinson's *Letters*.

p. 32 "No Elegy" is dedicated to A. B. Paulson.

p. 43 This poem is dedicated to Ann Riardon, who taught the disabled to dance.

About the Author

Irene McKinney was born in Belington, West Virginia, in 1939. She received her B.A. from West Virginia Wesleyan College, her M.A. from West Virginia University, and her Ph.D. from the University of Utah. She has taught poetry and literature at the University of California at Santa Cruz, the University of Utah, and Hamilton College. Her first book of poems, *The Girl with the Stone in Her Lap,* was published in 1976. It was followed by *The Wasps at the Blue Hexagons* (1984) and *Quick Fire and Slow Fire* (1988). Among her awards is a 1985 National Endowment for the Arts Poetry Fellowship. She lives in Belington, West Virginia.

PITT POETRY SERIES

Ed Ochester, General Editor